I0409483

Chapter I: A Chamber of Aspirations

Awakening to the soft caress of dawn's embrace, I find myself in the quietude of my modest abode. Sunbeams, gentle as a whisper, filter through the drapery, casting a warm glow upon my small chamber. It's no grandiose space, this room of mine, yet within its unassuming walls resides the entirety of my world.

Seated at my writing desk, I am enveloped by the familiar sanctuary that is my room. Bookshelves, laden with the weight of knowledge, stand as silent sentinels along the walls, their tomes awaiting the eager touch of exploration. A steadfast companion, my trusty computer, rests in the corner, a portal to the expansive realm of possibilities. An open notepad, its pages yearning to capture the ethereal dance of ideas that pirouette within my mind.

And then there is Sarah, a vivacious neighbor whose presence injects a lively vibrancy into my otherwise solitary world. She enters unbidden, bearing a tray adorned with the fragrant offerings of freshly baked cookies.

Sarah: (with cheer) "Greetings, denizen of the dwelling! I come bearing the sustenance of cookies, crafted to infuse vigor into your endeavors."

I find myself unable to resist the infectious enthusiasm that emanates from her being.

Alex: (expressing gratitude) "Sarah, your ability to illuminate even the dullest of days is a gift. I am genuinely thankful."

As we indulge in the warmth of the gooey confections, a sense of Sarah's inquisitiveness lingers in the air, mirroring the determination reflected in my gaze.

Sarah: (curious) "That look in your eyes, Alex—it speaks of ambitions. What schemes traverse the corridors of your ingenious mind today?"

Alex: (enthused) "Sarah, I have embarked on a journey into the realms of online commerce and entrepreneurship. I hold a profound belief that within the confines of this very room, I can amass a fortune."

Sarah: (intrigued) "A bold proclamation, indeed! Pray, elucidate your plan to manifest such aspirations."

Alex: (with conviction) "I have immersed myself in the study of investment strategies, the intricacies of online marketplaces, and the labyrinthine paths of e-commerce. Amidst this vast landscape, I am resolute in my quest to discover a niche that shall pave the way to affluence."

Sarah: (supportive) "Your determination is a beacon, Alex. I have faith in your journey, and your resolve is nothing short of inspiring."

Chapter II: The Ember of Ambition

Within the modest confines of my abode, a desk, laden with volumes, a vigilant computer, and an ever-present notepad, becomes the crucible of aspirations. A thirst for sagacity propels me into the realms of investment sagas, entrepreneurial sagas, and the expansive frontiers of online commerce.

As the sands of time sift through the hourglass, my tenacity remains unwavering. A sojourn through the digital maze reveals the latent potentials within the realm of online entrepreneurship, particularly the untouched reservoirs in the vast sea of e-commerce.

An epiphany strikes—a niche market, forsaken yet pregnant with possibilities. Guided by diligence, I embark on a meticulous pilgrimage, dissecting products, scrutinizing market trends, and etching a business manifesto. From the crucible of personal passions emerges a collection of handmade artisanal candles.

The sanctity of my quarters transforms into an ad-hoc studio, an arena of experimentation with waxes, scents, and designs. With a dedication bordering on obsession, I toil to birth candles that defy the commonplace, striving to carve a niche in the competitive market.

Despite adversities—a cascade of melted wax, the fragrance of setbacks, and the ceaseless dance of trial and error—my determination remains unbroken. Armed with the arsenal of social media, I leverage my burgeoning online presence. Each product photograph, each meticulously crafted description, becomes a brushstroke in painting a community around my brand.

Orders, akin to a gentle rain, commence a rhythmic tap at my digital threshold. Within the cozy confines of my abode, operations evolve into a bustling mini-factory. Specialized equipment finds its place, alliances with steadfast suppliers are forged, and a remote ensemble of artisans assembles for the ballet of packaging and dispatch.

With each dawn, revenues swell, and the dream of affluence inches closer. Profits, a pliable clay, mold the expansion of my product line, the diversification of offerings, and the refinement of the customer's journey.

Whispers of my triumph traverse the winds of entrepreneurial lore. I metamorphose into a symbol—a testament to resilience, a beacon of resourcefulness, an embodiment of the creed that unwavering determination births triumph. Entrepreneurs, a congregation from every compass point, seek my counsel, attend my virtual symposiums, and draw inspiration from the odyssey that is my tale.

Chapter III: Beyond the Chamber's Threshold

As the river of prosperity continues to flow, a profound realization begins to take root within me. While my humble chamber has served as the birthplace of wealth, a stirring desire to explore realms beyond its confined quarters begins to awaken. A yearning for connection with kindred spirits, a thirst to witness the grand tapestry of the world beyond, and a fervent drive to give back to the community that nurtured my ascent unfolds within my being.

Empowered by newfound confidence and an earnest aspiration to be a catalyst for positive change, I make the monumental decision to traverse the familiar boundaries of my room. Industry conferences become my gathering grounds, networking events my proving grounds, and mentors my guiding lights, steering the course of this extraordinary journey.

As my brand evolves into a global titan, a daring decision crystallizes—a physical store, strategically positioned in the pulsating heart of the city. A steadfast team, united by a shared vision, joins me in a collective mission to broaden our horizons.

Unsatisfied with mere success, my passion metamorphoses into a philanthropic venture. A foundation emerges, with a steadfast purpose: to bestow grants, mentorship, and resources upon aspiring entrepreneurs, particularly those grappling with the adversities of disadvantage. My journey transforms into a guiding beacon, extending its radiance not solely within the entrepreneurial realm but casting its glow to any soul yearning to transform dreams into tangible reality.

Within the vibrant embrace of the city, amid towering structures and bustling streets, a room transcends its physical dimensions. It becomes an emblem—an enduring symbol of perseverance, innovation, and the boundless potential embedded within every individual.

And thus, the chronicle of Alex—a seemingly ordinary individual who, within the sanctuary of a room, sculpted a realm of opportunity, ascended to millionaire status, and bestowed an enduring legacy as an inspiration for generations yet to unfold— reaches its crescendo.

Chapter IV: Trials and Triumphs

As the dominion of my brand expands, so do the trials that accompany the journey. The room, erstwhile a haven of aspirations, now stands witness to the rigors and trials inherent in the business arena.

What was once a sanctum of boundless dreams transforms into a chamber where late-night contemplations and fervent strategy sessions unfold. The bookshelves, once adorned with volumes of knowledge, now bear the weight not just of wisdom but also of financial reports, marketing blueprints, and echoes of customer sentiments.

On an evening steeped in the quietude of my desk, burdened by stacks of invoices and the contemplation of pivotal decisions, Sarah makes a timely entrance.

Sarah: (with concern) "Alex, I've noticed your ceaseless endeavors. You haven't taken a respite in weeks. You appear fatigued."

Alex: (weary) "The pace of growth is unyielding, Sarah. There's no room for deceleration. I must persist."

Sarah: (supportive) "Dedication is commendable, but even the most triumphant entrepreneurs necessitate moments of reprieve. Burnout serves no purpose."

With the passage of time, the room, once an abode of inspiration, begins to feel like a cage. The walls, silent witnesses to my endeavors, now reverberate with the strains of mounting pressures and burgeoning responsibilities. The flame of purpose within me persists, unwavering, yet an unseen burden settles upon my shoulders, casting shadows in what was once an illuminated sanctuary.

Chapter V: The Depths of Despair

Within the sacred confines of my chamber, a day unfolds heavy with the burdens of my business realm. The room, once a sanctuary of inspiration, now echoes with the somber notes of disillusionment.

Alex:
(frustrated) "Success, it seems, has brought forth a torrent of unforeseen challenges. This room, once a refuge, now stands as a fortress, Sarah."

Sarah: (sympathetic) "It's natural to feel the weight, Alex. Reflect on the core of your journey. It surpasses mere financial triumph; it's about nurturing your passion."

Alex: (reflective) "Your words bear truth, Sarah. I must chart a course back to the essence of what truly matters."

In the abyss of my lowest ebb, a formidable decision looms. Temporarily closing the physical store emerges as a necessary act, a respite that allows me to reassess priorities and reignite the flames of my passion. It is a moment of introspection, seeking solace in the timeless principles that have guided my journey thus far.

Chapter VI: The Sentinel's Stare

In the resurgence of my brand, a new ordeal emerges, casting its shadow over the landscape of success. The allure of my achievements becomes a siren call, beckoning competitors who, in their pursuit, stoop to unscrupulous stratagems.

One day, an enigmatic missive arrives, carrying clandestine insights into the inner workings of my upcoming ventures and marketing maneuvers.

Alex: (concerned) "Sarah, this missive—its contents are privy solely to our inner circle."

Sarah: (worried) "This is ominous, Alex. Someone endeavors to cast shadows upon your enterprise."

Initiating an inquiry, with the expertise of a cybersecurity adept, a disconcerting revelation unfolds—my computer stands violated. Corporate espionage, a venomous serpent, reveals its sinister coils.

Alex: (determined) "We cannot permit this subterfuge. Action is imperative to shield our enterprise."

Sarah: (resolute) "Let us pursue these malefactors and ensure they face the consequences of their deeds, for no shadow shall cloak the light of our endeavors."

Chapter VII: The Battle for Equity

Armed with the irrefutable evidence I've amassed, I resolve to wage a legal war against the perpetrators of the cyber onslaught. It unfolds as a protracted and taxing ordeal, extracting a toll not only on my emotional resilience but also on the coffers that sustain my enterprise.

The room, once a sanctuary of dreams, morphs into a battleground for justice. Legal parchments and court proceedings inundate my desk, and the luxury of restful nights becomes a distant memory.

Sarah: (supportive) "This is an uphill struggle, Alex, but we must not allow them to evade accountability."

Alex: (determined) "Your wisdom is evident, Sarah. We shall persist in our pursuit of justice, undeterred by the tribulations."

Empowered by unyielding determination, I emerge victorious. The wrongdoers face the consequences of their actions, and my brand, tempered by the fires of adversity, emerges from the crucible stronger and more resilient than ever before.

Chapter VIII: Governmental Tribulations and Fiscal Quandaries

In the shadow of success, the government's gaze sharpens, and tax authorities unfurl a scrutiny that blankets the financial landscape of my enterprise, heralding a succession of audits and inquiries.

Alex: (frustrated) "It seems they aim to unearth flaws in every corner of our business, Sarah."

Sarah: (concerned) "Fear not, Alex. Let us seek the counsel of a tax expert to navigate this labyrinth."

The room metamorphoses into a repository for tax scrolls and financial scrolls, as my team and I toil tirelessly to harmonize with the intricate cadence of tax regulations. It proves to be a taxing epoch, yet our dedication to transparency and integrity stands as a steadfast guide, leading us through the convoluted corridors of governmental scrutiny.

Chapter IX: Triumph and Prosperity

Amidst the tempest of challenges, setbacks, and moments of uncertain resolve, my chamber metamorphoses into an emblem of resilience. Forged through trials and fueled by unwavering determination, I conquer obstacles once deemed insurmountable.

With the specters of cyber adversity and tax trials vanquished, my brand ascends to new heights. The room, a silent witness to the undulating waves of my journey, once again reverberates with the energy of innovation and anticipation.

I diversify my product array, venture into unexplored markets, and carve an indomitable niche in the industry. The room, adorned not only with the wisdom of books but also bedecked with the tangible symbols of success—awards and accolades—stands as a testament to the enduring fortitude that propelled me through the tumultuous voyage.

Chapter X: The Evolution of the Chamber

As the sands of time cascade, a transformation unfolds within the room. No longer a chaotic workspace, it blossoms into a haven of inspiration and ingenuity. A designated nook becomes the canvas for collaborative brainstorming sessions, where ideas dance freely among my team.

The walls, once silent witnesses to trials, now wear the adornments of a vision board—a mosaic of images and notes portraying the boundless expanses of our dreams. The room, in its evolution, mirrors my odyssey—a journey that not only sculpts my destiny but intertwines its essence with those who share this sacred space.

Henceforth, from the heart of an unassuming room in a bustling city, my legacy weaves its enduring narrative of inspiration. My sojourn stands as a living testament to the potency of perseverance, innovation, and unyielding determination. The room itself, now a symbol of limitless potential, stands as an affirmation that within its confines, dreams can take root and flourish, undeterred by the challenges that may lay ahead.

Chapter XI: The Concealed Battle

As my chamber retained its role as the epicenter of an expanding empire, the burden of responsibility swelled. The murmurs of triumph and admiration from the external world stealthily took root in my psyche, giving rise to an ego hitherto uncharted.

Alex (reflecting): *I've traversed vast distances, achieved immeasurable feats. Invincibility is my ally.*

Once fleeting, these self-assured reflections transformed into a constant companion, veiled within the shadows. With adept artistry, I concealed my burgeoning ego, shielding it from the discerning gaze of those around me, especially Sarah.

Sarah (expressing concern): "Alex, you've seemed distant lately. Is everything in order?"

Alex (feigning nonchalance): "Certainly, Sarah. Just grappling with the routine challenges of business."

Yet, beneath the facade of assurance, a tempest brewed. The swelling ego beckoned me to embrace greater risks, prioritize personal desires above all, and revel in the radiance of my triumphs. Slowly, insidiously, I drifted toward narcissism, heedless of the toll it exacted on relationships and the fragile equilibrium of my own inner world.

Chapter XII: The Mirage of Deceit

In tandem with the inflation of my ego, my skill in the art of deception burgeoned, especially in the eyes of Sarah. I couldn't bear the thought of her witnessing the metamorphosis within me—the burgeoning arrogance, the swelling self-absorption threatening to overshadow my very essence.

Sarah (expressing concern): "Alex, decisions are being made without consulting the team. This isn't the Alex I know."

Alex (defensive): "I discern what's optimal for the business, Sarah. I can't afford to tarry for others to catch up."

In verity, I had succumbed to the delusion that I alone propelled our success. The conviction of the superiority of my ideas and the infallibility of my decisions held me in thrall.

One day, Sarah confronted me, her words laden with apprehension.

Sarah (directly): "Alex, you've undergone a transformation. This isn't the person I once knew. Arrogance and dismissal have replaced humility."

Alex (feigning innocence): "To guide the business, assertiveness is imperative, Sarah. The world is unforgiving."

Yet, the words rang hollow—a deceptive veil concealing the ego's grip on me. The humble and resolute individual who embarked on this odyssey was now a mere specter. In his stead stood a narcissist, blinded by the reflection of his own success.

Chapter XIII: The Veil of Solitude

In the swell of my triumphs, a subtle yet profound shift took root —a growing distance between myself and those who once shared the journey. Sarah, a trusted companion, confronted me with the poignant pain of our diminishing bond.

"Alex, there was a time when you would confide in me. We were a team. Now, it feels like you don't even listen," her words echoed with the resonance of a connection slipping away.

In response, my retort carried a hint of defensiveness, "Sarah, I'm steering a business, not running a support group."

The weight of isolation became increasingly apparent. Enveloped in the grandeur of my achievements, I remained blind to the encroaching solitude that silently infiltrated my life. The success I fervently pursued exacted a toll—a toll measured in the fading echoes of human connection.

Chapter XIV: The Awakening

In the chronicles of my entrepreneurial saga, a pivotal chapter unfolded—a chapter marked not by triumph but by a resounding setback that echoed through the corridors of my business empire. The blow, both unexpected and formidable, shattered the illusion of invincibility I had meticulously crafted.

Seated amidst the debris of shattered dreams and wounded pride, Sarah, a steadfast companion, once again graced the sanctuary of my room. Her demeanor bore a blend of concern and an unyielding resolve.

Sarah (resolutely): "Alex, the hour of reckoning is upon us. Your ego, once a silent accomplice, has now become the architect of discord, not only between us but within your very being."

Alex (weary): "I am a stranger to myself, Sarah. The siren call of success... it has transformed me."

Sarah (encouraging): "Yet, change is a realm within reach, Alex. It is never too late to navigate the path of redemption. Mistakes, though inevitable, serve as the crucible from which profound lessons emerge."

Chapter XV: The Path to Redemption

In the annals of my narrative, a chapter unfolded—the tale of a journey towards self-redemption, guided by the unwavering compass of Sarah's support. The road ahead proved challenging, for it demanded a confrontation with the narcissistic tendrils that had coiled around my character. Yet, with a resolute spirit, I committed to the task of rediscovering the person I once knew.

Therapy and counseling emerged as my stalwart companions on this odyssey. Together, we navigated the intricate passages of my ego, unraveling the threads that wove the tapestry of narcissism. The expedition was not without its tribulations, each session akin to a lantern casting light into the shadowy recesses of my insecurities and fears—revealing the very roots that had fostered my profound metamorphosis.

Chapter XVI: The Rebirth of Humility

In the silent corridors of time, a chapter unfolded—a narrative of reconnection and redemption. The threads of reconciliation, especially with my team and the pivotal figure of Sarah, wove a tapestry of sincere apologies and earnest amends.

A profound truth revealed itself—an understanding that the metric of true success transcended the grandiosity of one's ego. Instead, it found its essence in the benevolent impact one could impart upon others and the vast canvas of the world.

Sarah (forgiving): "Alex, your return to humility is a balm to our collective spirit. We longed for the essence of the person you once embodied."

Alex (grateful): "Sarah, your steadfast support has been the compass guiding me through this transformative odyssey. I am profoundly thankful."

Chapter XVII: A Genesis of Renewal

As the shadows of ego and narcissism relinquished their hold, my room underwent a profound metamorphosis. It ceased to be a bastion of isolation and deceit, emerging instead as a sanctuary infused with the virtues of humility and personal growth.

Empowered by the invaluable lessons garnered from the crucible of self-discovery, I charted a new course for my business. Its trajectory realigned with the pure essence of its founding mission —to craft products that not only kindled joy but also contributed substantive value to the intricate fabric of people's lives. Reconnecting with my team, we embarked on a collective journey, fortified in our shared commitment to surmount the challenges that lay on the horizon

Chapter XVIII: The Legacy of Enduring Wisdom

As the final pages unfurled, the chronicle of my odyssey from the clutches of ego to the embrace of humility resonated as a testament—a legacy etched in enduring wisdom.

The room, once an emblem of solitude, transformed into a sanctum of reflection and metamorphosis. It bore witness to the profound truth that authentic success, adorned with the mantle of humility, resonated with the deepest chords of significance.

Thus, my story persisted—a narrative no longer entwined with the threads of ego and narcissism but evolved into a parable extolling the timeless virtues of character development, self-discovery, and an unwavering commitment to the authentic self. The legacy of enduring wisdom, now engraved in the fabric of my journey, served as a guiding light for those who would traverse similar paths, beckoning them towards the richness of a life well-lived.

Chapter XIX: The Unveiling Shadows

In the corridors of prosperity, where success cast its benevolent light, shadows emerged to challenge the very bonds forged in the crucible of entrepreneurship. Max, a steadfast companion in the arduous journey of building our brand, now stood accused of betraying the sacred trust that had been the cornerstone of our shared aspirations.

The ledgers, once pristine chronicles of financial endeavors, bore witness to a disconcerting reality—substantial sums surreptitiously siphoned from the coffers, an ominous revelation of Max's covert transgressions.

Alex (perplexed): "How swiftly can the pillars of trust crumble, Sarah? Max was not merely a collaborator; he was a friend, a confidant."

Sarah (aghast): "Deception, Alex, assumes myriad guises. Now, we must confront this betrayal and chart a course toward restoration."

Chapter XX: The Abyss Beckons

The tremors of betrayal resonated within the chamber of my once-vibrant aspirations. The sanctuary that housed dreams now stood tainted with the ink of deception, casting shadows upon the very essence of trust.

Alex (whispering in despair): "In this room where dreams took flight, a sinister specter now lingers. How did the bonds of trust unravel, Sarah?"

Sarah (sympathetic): "Even the strongest foundations can crumble, Alex. It's in rebuilding that we find our true strength."

Yet, the room, once a haven, transformed into a chasm of desolation. Each step echoed with the weight of Max's deceit, leaving a palpable void in the air. The financial records, once a testament to shared endeavors, now chronicled the unraveling partnership.

Alex (contemplative): "In this abyss, where camaraderie once thrived, I'm left to ponder the remnants of what was. Can trust, once shattered, ever mend?"

Chapter XXI: The Arduous Path to Restoration

In the crucible of adversity, where shadows of betrayal cast their ominous silhouette, I sought solace within the hallowed chambers of therapy. The room, once resonant with despair, now echoed with the whispers of redemption.

Therapist (with sagacity): "Healing, dear Alex, is akin to sculpting from the remnants of trust. Begin by forgiving yourself, for trust, once fractured, requires the mending touch of self-compassion."

Enlightened by the therapeutic verses, I embarked on a journey of reconstruction—both of my shattered spirit and the tattered tapestry of trust. The room, witness to my tribulations, transformed into a crucible of resilience and introspection.

Alex (contemplative): "While I can't govern the actions of others, I hold sway over my response. The room need not merely echo betrayal; it can reverberate with the cadence of my ascent."

Guided by the therapist's sagacious counsel and fortified by the steadfast companionship of Sarah, I embraced vulnerability as the cornerstone of my rejuvenation. The room, once enshrouded in shadows, bore witness to the genesis of a more robust and self-aware self.

Sarah (supportive): "Alex, trust isn't about obliterating the past; it's about forging a resolute path forward. Let the room echo not just with the whispers of betrayal but with the triumphant cadence of your resilience."

As the odyssey of reconstruction unfolded, the room metamorphosed into a metaphor—an allegory for the indomitable human spirit, capable of enduring, learning, and emerging from the shadows with newfound strength.

The room offered no solace, becoming a silent witness to the intricate dance of emotions—pain, reflection, and the flicker of resilience in the face of adversity. In the depths of this abyss, a glimmer of strength awaited, poised to guide a phoenix rising from the ashes of betrayal.

Chapter XXII: The Tenuous Threads

In the aftermath of betrayal's tempest, Sarah emerged as an unwavering beacon, yet even the foundation of our camaraderie bore the indelible marks of my struggle with trust.

Sarah (with a gentle plea): "Alex, I stand by you, but trust is the fragile filament that binds friendships. Without it, we exist in the shadows of doubt."

Alex (apologetically): "Sarah, I am earnestly trying. The echoes of Max's betrayal resonate, casting shadows even on the bonds we once held unshakable."

Our exchanges, once harmonious symphonies, now bore the dissonance of unspoken apprehensions. Within my being, a fervent yearning kindled—an aspiration to mend not only the frayed connections with others but to weave anew the very fabric of self-trust.

Chapter XXIII: The Voyage of Renewal

Amidst the crucible of therapeutic introspection and the patient passage of time, I embarked upon an ascending trajectory from the profound depths of despair. The room, a silent witness to my darkest hours, now stood as a monument to an incremental renaissance.

Alex (resolute): "I refuse to be ensnared by the shadows of betrayal, Sarah. The time has come to resurrect my trust, both in others and in the sanctum of my own character."

Sarah (encouraging): "You're steering in the right direction, Alex. We shall navigate this odyssey one measured step at a time."

Commencing the reconstruction, I fortified the foundations of my business, distilling invaluable insights from the crucible of betrayal. The erection of safeguards became paramount, constructing an impregnable bulwark against potential malfeasance. The scars etched into the tapestry of my journey persisted, tangible emblems underscoring the profound significance of trust and the indomitable spirit intrinsic to the voyage of recovery.

Chapter XXIV: The Journey

of Atonement

As the delicate threads of trust began to mend, so too did the intricate weaving of my connection with Sarah. Within the crucible of shared vulnerabilities, we laid bare the fabric of our fears and aspirations.

Sarah (compassionate): "To witness your willingness to unveil, Alex, is heartening. Redemption doesn't lie in the absence of mistakes but in the earnest endeavor to learn and evolve."

Alex (appreciative): "Your steadfast presence, Sarah, has been the bedrock of my resilience. I am truly grateful for your unwavering support through this intricate odyssey."

Chapter XXV: The Dawn of Renewal

As the seasons changed, so did the aura within my chamber. It ceased to be a witness to solitude and despair; instead, it transformed into a sanctuary of rejuvenation and growth. The wounds inflicted by betrayal and the battles against depression and anxiety became not shackles but stepping stones, propelling me toward a more robust and enduring spirit.

Armed with the hard-won wisdom gained through adversity, I reached out with a compassionate hand to those traversing similar tribulations. My journey, from the clutches of betrayal to the rekindling of hope, became a guiding light, illuminating the unique paths that others could tread on their quest for redemption.

Chapter XXVI: The Legacy of Resilience

In the tapestry of my journey, woven with threads of challenges and triumphs, the room stood as a silent witness to the transformation that had unfolded within its walls. No longer a chamber of despair, it emerged as a sanctuary of hope and renewal.

The narrative transcended the mere saga of business conquests; it evolved into a parable of fortitude, the capacity to navigate the shadows and emerge enlightened. The room, a once-haunted testament to betrayal, now radiated the essence of human resilience and growth.

Through the ebb and flow of adversity, my legacy etched itself not just in the ledgers of prosperity but in the annals of overcoming, a beacon for those navigating their own tumultuous seas. As the room bore witness, it symbolized the indomitable spirit to rise stronger from the crucible of tribulations—a testament to the enduring legacy of resilience.

Chapter XXVII: The Desire to Give Back

Amidst the evolving chapters of my life, a profound yearning stirred—a call to contribute to the community and offer guidance to aspiring entrepreneurs, particularly those grappling with the challenges of disadvantage. My journey, marked by triumphs and tribulations, had cultivated a reservoir of knowledge, and the urge to share these lessons burned within me.

Workshops and mentorship initiatives emerged as vessels through which I could extend a helping hand to fellow entrepreneurs navigating their unique voyages. Within the confines of my room, once a sanctuary for personal pursuits, a transformation occurred—a shift towards becoming a wellspring of inspiration, resonating with the melodies of dreams taking flight and the boundless possibilities of entrepreneurial endeavors.

Chapter XXVIII: The First

Signs of Discord

As I extended my hand to uplift others, the path was not without obstacles. Skepticism and resistance emerged, casting shadows upon my genuine intentions. Accusations of ulterior motives and profit-seeking pierced the air, turning the once-warm embrace of assistance into a chilly rebuff.

Alex (confused): "Sarah, why do they question my motives? All I desire is to genuinely help."

Sarah (reflective): "Understanding intentions takes time, Alex. Stay true to your purpose; sincerity has its way of shining through."

Chapter XXIX: The Growing Hostility

In the noble pursuit of benevolence, the shadows of hostility began to loom, casting doubt upon my sincere endeavors. Whispers of accusation, like the sinister rustle of leaves in a dark forest, painted me as a manipulative opportunist, allegedly intent on exploiting the dreams of others.

Entrepreneur (accusatory): "You're just using us for your own gain, Alex. We don't need your charity."

Alex (wounded): "That's not true! I'm trying to make a positive impact."

The arrows of mistrust, sharp and unforgiving, found their mark, piercing the armor of good intentions. Such attacks on my character wounded me deeply, prompting a retreat to the sanctuary of my room—a refuge where I could shield myself from the harsh judgments and, undeterred, channel my focus into the meaningful work that defined my purpose.

Chapter XXX: The Self-Reflection

In the gentle echoes of Sarah's counsel, resonated the wisdom of self-reflection. Her supportive words became a compass, guiding me through the labyrinth of unintended consequences.

Sarah (supportive): "Alex, perhaps it's time to take a step back and assess how you're coming across to others. We can work on your approach together."

Alex (introspective): "You're right, Sarah. Maybe I've been too focused on helping without considering how it's being received."

In the quiet confines of my room, the sanctum of contemplation, I embarked on a journey of introspection. It was a moment to acknowledge that my fervent desire to make a positive impact might have inadvertently cast shadows of suspicion. With newfound clarity, I vowed to refine my approach, ensuring that my benevolent intentions harmonized with the perceptions of those I sought to assist.

Chapter XXXI: The Humble Approach

In the grand theater of redemption, the stage was set for a humble overture. Acknowledging the dissonance that echoed in the hearts of those who questioned, I took center stage.

Alex (apologetic): "I understand why some of you may be wary of my assistance. I'm here to learn and improve."

With sincerity as my script and humility as my costume, I endeavored to bridge the gap between intent and perception. The room, witness to many chapters, now stood witness to the unfolding drama of transformation.

Chapter XXXII: The Gradual Reconciliation

As the hourglass of time continued its measured descent, the seeds of humility and sincerity I sowed began to sprout, mending the fractures of distrust. The skeptics, once entrenched in doubt, now glimpsed the authenticity beneath my actions.

Entrepreneur (grateful): "I misjudged you, Alex. Thank you for your support and guidance."

The room, a silent witness to the ebb and flow of human dynamics, observed the deliberate steps of reconciliation—a dance where understanding pirouetted in tandem with gratitude.

Chapter XXXIII: The Virtue of Humility

In the crucible of challenges, I forged a virtue rare—humility, a jewel of character polished by the abrasive sands of public perception. The journey, laden with judgments and skepticism, unveiled the profundity of self-awareness and the necessity of bowing before the wisdom embedded in humility's embrace.

As I walked the path of redemption, each step resonated with the echoes of humility's quiet strength. It wasn't merely a cloak worn for appearances; it became the very fabric of my being. Sarah, a constant guide in this transformative odyssey, witnessed the evolution.

Sarah (wise): "Humility isn't a surrender of strength, Alex. It's a mastery of the self, a recognition that true influence sprouts from understanding and empathy."

And so, I learned to listen, not with the intent to respond, but with the genuine curiosity to comprehend. The room, once witness to hostility, now hosted conversations drenched in humility's soothing balm.

As my endeavors to assist and uplift persisted, the virtue of humility stood sentinel, guarding against the arrogance that had once tarnished my intentions. Each entrepreneur I encountered became a mirror, reflecting the nuanced contours of their aspirations, fears, and dreams.

In humility's embrace, bridges were built where chasms had yawned. Entrepreneurs, once skeptical, found solace in the sincerity of purpose. It was not about asserting influence; it was about extending a hand with the authentic desire to uplift.

The virtue of humility, etched into the narrative of my journey, transcended the realm of personal growth—it became the cornerstone of genuine connection and transformative impact. And so, with each chapter, humility emerged as the quiet yet formidable protagonist, steering the course of my endeavors toward a horizon where sincerity and understanding reigned supreme.

Chapter XXXIV: The Continued Efforts

In the silent sanctum of my room, a renewed spirit of humility guided my ongoing endeavors in mentoring and supporting aspiring entrepreneurs. The lessons of the past sculpted a refined approach, one that embraced transparency and authenticity as the pillars of trust.

No longer driven solely by an eagerness to assist, I navigated the delicate intricacies of perception. The room, once an arena of skepticism, now resonated with the sincerity of purpose and the measured tones of guidance.

Alex (contemplative): "In mentorship, every word carries weight, and every action shapes perception. It's not just about what I offer; it's about how it's received."

Sarah, my steadfast companion in this transformative journey, observed the shift—a metamorphosis where influence emanated not just from assertiveness but from a profound understanding.

Sarah (appreciative): "Your continued efforts reveal a depth of wisdom, Alex. It's a testament to the transformative power of self-awareness."

The entrepreneurs, recipients of this evolved mentorship, discovered not just guidance but an authentic connection. The legacy of my journey, now interwoven with the virtue of humility, unfolded as a guiding light for those traversing the maze of aspirations.

And so, with each persistent endeavor, the room echoed with the harmonies of shared dreams—a symphony composed with the virtuosity of humility, resonating through the corridors of entrepreneurial ambitions.

Chapter XXXV: The Legacy of Resilience and Redemption

In the sacred precincts of my abode, the chronicle unfolds —a parable of unwavering tenacity, self-awareness, and the paramount significance of actions over mere intentions. No more a haven of solitude and desolation, it emerges anew—a symbol of optimism, metamorphosis, and the indomitable essence of evolution.

The legacy I weave stretches far beyond the contours of business conquests, crafting a narrative interwoven with the threads of fortitude and modesty. From the wreckage of trust's demise, a narrative of reclamation surfaces—a testimony to the extraordinary faculty of healing fractured bonds. My chamber, once a passive spectator to discord, now reverberates with a profound verity—the human spirit's resilience for revival and the potent force embedded in the waves of constructive transformation.

Chapter XXXVI: The Yearning for Acceptance

As the tapestry of my triumphs continued to unfurl, an insatiable yearning took root—the hunger for acknowledgment amidst the echelons of entrepreneurs and titans of industry. The desire for validation echoed in the corridors of my ambition, a conviction that their recognition would serve as the ultimate imprimatur on my endeavors.

Alex (resolute): "I aspire to stand among the paragons, Sarah. Acceptance by the elite is the pinnacle I aim to ascend."

Sarah (cautionary): "Alex, remember your roots and the principles that ushered you here."

Yet, my resolve remained unyielding. I graced exclusive galas and networking soirees, eagerly seeking to etch my name into the annals of the elite. However, the stark realization soon descended upon me—my origins and upbringing bestowed upon me a distinctiveness I had not foreseen.

Chapter XXXVII: The Elusive Acceptance

Within the echelons of the elite, a subtle dance of disdain unfolded, casting shadows upon the fruits of my earnest labor. Their veiled mockery reduced my achievements to mere happenstance.

Elite Entrepreneur (condescending): "Ah, the dweller of that unassuming chamber, is it not? Engaging in the theatrics of entrepreneurship, I presume."

Alex (resolute): "My endeavors are born of ceaseless dedication. My origins neither diminish nor define the merit of my pursuits."

Yet, my impassioned retort echoed in an indifferent chamber. The elite's skepticism endured, a persistent reminder of the profound gulf that separated our worlds. The coveted acceptance I yearned for remained a spectral mirage, eluding my grasp.

Chapter XXXVIII: The Emotional Toll

The corridors of elite approval, strewn with the remnants of rejection, exacted an emotional toll that reverberated within the chambers of my being. Despite the tapestry of achievements woven through dedication, their disdain left me ensnared in the tendrils of inadequacy.

Sarah (steadfast): "Alex, your success stands independent of their recognition. You've forged a path uniquely yours."

Alex (frustrated): "I understand, but the sting of being an outsider among them is hard to shake."

Thus, my room, once a sanctuary of inspiration, now echoed with the disquieting whispers of self-doubt, a poignant reminder of the unattained validation I sought among the elite.

Chapter XXXIX: The Inner Struggle

Within the labyrinth of my emotions, a tempest raged—a conflict between the ardent desire for acceptance among the elite and the realization that their acknowledgment should not be the measure of my inherent value.

Alex (introspective): "Why does their opinion matter so much, Sarah? I should take pride in my journey and origins."

Sarah (wise): "The quest for acceptance is innate, Alex, but not at the expense of your intrinsic worth."

Chapter XL: The Reevaluation

Amidst the echoes of contemplation, I discerned a profound truth. My triumphs were woven from the fabric of authenticity and the steadfast embrace of cherished values. I stood at a crossroads, grappling with the realization that the opinions of the elite should not cast a shadow over the essence of my journey.

Alex (resolute): "I shall not trade my authenticity for their acceptance, Sarah. My path will remain true to the values that define me."

Sarah (proud): "In staying true to yourself, Alex, you illuminate a path that others may follow. Your journey is a testament to authenticity and resilience."

Chapter XLI: The New Perspective

Amidst the ebb and flow of passing days, a transformation stirred within my being. Liberated from the ceaseless pursuit of elite acknowledgment, my focus pivoted towards a profound epiphany. My vigor, once fixated on the allure of prestige, now found purpose in the noble art of mentoring and uplifting kindred spirits tethered, much like myself, to modest origins.

Alex (passionate): "Let the chronicles of my odyssey illuminate the path, inspiring others to wear their roots as badges of honor, irrespective of humble beginnings."

Sarah (supportive): "Your vision is laudable, Alex. Through the narrative of your journey, you plant seeds of inspiration that possess the potential to sprout into profound transformation."

Chapter XLII: The Legacy of Authenticity

As the sands of time drifted, my chronicle unfolded as a testament to the enduring power of authenticity, self-acceptance, and the profound significance of staying tethered to one's roots. Within the confines of my chamber, a sanctuary that bore witness to the ebb and flow of transformation, a narrative blossomed—a living parable of the strength found in embracing one's true self.

And so, my legacy surpassed the fleeting desire for acknowledgment from the elite; it metamorphosed into a fable, an ode to celebrating one's identity and kindling a flame of inspiration in the hearts of others. My room, once shrouded in the shadows of self-doubt, emerged as a symbol—an enduring testimony to the intrinsic value embedded in authenticity.

Chapter XLIII: The Unpredictable Forces

In the ongoing tapestry of my odyssey, unforeseen challenges emerged, formidable in their essence—nature's whims, the undulating tides of the economy, and the capricious dance of global events. These unpredictable forces loomed, casting shadows of uncertainty upon my business and existence.

Alex (perturbed): "Sarah, it seems as though we are but pawns in the hands of these unpredictable forces. How do we navigate this labyrinth of uncertainty?"

Sarah (undaunted): "We adapt, Alex. In the crucible of adversity, we've forged resilience before, and we shall chart a course through this tempest as well."

Chapter XLIV: The Tempest of Uncertainty

In the grand saga of my ventures, a formidable trial emerged—a tempest born of nature's fury, an unforeseen hurricane that laid waste to our production haven. The room, witness to triumphs past, now stood in the shadows of devastation.

Alex (bereft): "All that we painstakingly crafted... obliterated, Sarah."

Sarah (steadfast): "We shall rebuild, Alex. In the echoes of adversity, resilience shall sculpt anew, as it has done in times bygone."

Chapter XLV: The Economic Turmoil

In the chronicles of our endeavors, the ominous shadow of economic upheaval materialized—a global recession, a tempest that cast shadows on consumer purses. Our once-soaring sales descended into the abyss, and the room, once a haven of innovation, now echoed with the whispers of uncertainty.

Alex (anxious): "Finances are hemorrhaging, Sarah. I fear for how much longer we can endure."

Sarah (steadfast): "We shall cinch our belts, trim the excess, and brave this turbulence. Our mettle has been tested in the crucible of adversity before."

Chapter XLVI: The Pandemic's Arrival

In the vast tapestry of our narrative, a chapter unfolded unforeseen—an epoch marked by the advent of a global pandemic. A relentless force, it birthed lockdowns, disrupted supply chains, and shrouded us in an atmosphere of profound vulnerability.

Alex (apprehensive): "The world seems inverted, Sarah. How do we navigate these uncharted waters and ensure the survival of our business?"

Sarah (soothing): "Adaptation is our compass, Alex. We'll chart new courses to reach our customers and safeguard our team amidst the turbulence."

Chapter XLVII: The Emotional Toll

In the grand tapestry of trials, a solemn movement unfolds—a chapter etched with the toll of forces beyond mortal command. The room, erstwhile a sanctuary of inspiration, now resonates with the melancholy of frustration and uncertainty.

Alex (weary): "Sleep eludes me, Sarah. The weight of these uncontrollable forces is a burden too heavy."

Sarah (compassionate): "I empathize, Alex. Yet, endure we shall, just as we have weathered storms in times bygone."

Chapter XLVIII: The Power of Resilience

In the crucible of adversity, a profound testament to the strength of the human spirit emerges. The room, once echoing with the symphony of innovation, now narrates a tale of hard choices, adaptive transformations, and the forging of unyielding resolve.

Alex (undaunted): "Against these unrelenting forces, we remain steadfast, Sarah. Surrender is not an option; our journey has been too formidable to succumb now."

Sarah (hopeful): "The room may bear scars, but it stands defiant. So do we."

Chapter XLIX: The Resurgence

Amid the remnants of challenges conquered, a resurgence begins to unfold. The room, witness to the ebb and flow of fortune, becomes a sanctuary for rebirth and renewed vigor.

Alex (resilient): "We've weathered storms and risen from the ashes. This room, like our spirit, embodies the essence of resurgence."

Sarah (steadfast): "Our journey persists, Alex. With every trial, we emerge stronger, and this room stands as a testament to our resilience."

Chapter LI: The Ebbing Passion

As the years unfolded and my business reached new heights,

an unexpected adversary emerged—an erosion of the fervent motivation that once fueled my every endeavor. The room, a silent witness to triumphs and trials, now harbors a subtle emptiness.

Alex (reflective): "Sarah, there was a time when every sunrise brought new ideas and fresh enthusiasm. Now, it's a struggle to find that same spark."

Sarah (empathetic): "Motivation, like the tides, has its ebbs and flows. Together, we'll navigate these waters and rekindle the flames."

Chapter LII: The Burden of Triumph

As the echelons of success unfolded before me, I grappled with an unexpected burden—the weight of accomplishments that had once driven me. The room, witness to aspirations turned reality, now echoed with the subtle strain of this newfound success.

Alex (introspective): "Sarah, I believed success would be an unending wellspring of motivation. Yet, it feels like I've reached a summit, and the path forward is unclear."

Sarah (guiding): "Let's explore new horizons, Alex. Perhaps a deeper purpose lies beyond the peaks you've already conquered."

Chapter LIII: The Quest for Significance

In the chambers of introspection, I embarked on a quest to unveil a more profound purpose, one that could breathe new life into my dwindling motivation. The room, once resonating with the triumphant echoes of success, now echoed with the silent stirrings of this inner exploration.

Alex (contemplative): "Sarah, the summit of success hasn't provided the fulfillment I sought. There must be a path to leave a meaningful imprint."

Sarah (insightful): "Let's delve into the core of your passions, Alex. Therein lies the key to crafting a legacy that transcends mere financial triumph."

Chapter LIV: The Harmony Within

In the labyrinth of conflicting priorities, I embarked on a journey to rediscover equilibrium. The room, a silent witness to the struggles within, yearned for the cadence of harmony to permeate its walls.

Alex (resolute): "Balance is the true art of life, Sarah. I must synchronize the rhythm of my busine
ss with the melody of a meaningful legacy."

Sarah (assuring): "Together, we shall compose this symphony, Alex. Your odyssey will echo the harmonious blend of purpose and prosperity."

Chapter LV: The Cyclical Essence

In the rhythmic dance of my entrepreneurial odyssey, I uncovered the cyclical nature of motivation. The room, a silent witness to the undulating tides of inspiration, cradled the understanding that the flame of motivation, akin to the changing seasons, experiences cycles of waxing and waning.

Alex (reflective): "Motivation, much like the seasons, has its rhythm. It's about embracing the cycles and drawing strength from the inevitable changes."

Sarah (supportive): "The room has seen us through many seasons, Alex. It stands as a silent guardian of our journey's natural cadence."

Chapter LVI: The Revitalized Spirit

In the quiet chambers of my room, a renewed energy echoed

through the air. It became a sanctuary where the lessons of the past harmonized with the aspirations of the future.

Alex (reinvigorated): "This room, a silent witness to the cycles of motivation, now stands as a testament to resilience. It's a compass guiding me through the ever-evolving chapters."

Sarah (reflective): "May the forthcoming chapters be adorned with the harmony of purpose, and may the enduring dance of motivation lead us to new horizons."

Chapter LVII: The Legacy of Adaptation

In the labyrinth of life's twists and turns, I discovered the profound art of adaptation. The room, once a silent spectator to the shifts in motivation, now stood as a testament to the resilience inherent in our ability to change and grow.

Alex (reflective): "Life's journey is a dance of adaptation, Sarah. Our legacy is shaped not by the challenges we face, but by how we respond to them."

Sarah (contemplative): "Indeed, Alex. The room echoes the melody of your adaptation, a timeless song of growth and renewal."

Chapter LVIII: Glimpses of the Future

As the tapestry of my achievements unfolded, the room became a sanctuary for reflection, a space where I could contemplate the yet unwritten chapters of my journey. The past, a prelude to the mysteries of the future, beckoned me to explore the uncharted territories that lay beyond the horizon.

Alex (reflective): "The road ahead is shrouded in uncertainty, Sarah. As I gaze into the future, I sense the yearning for new beginnings, perhaps the embrace of family to accompany the unwritten tales."

Sarah (optimistic): "The future is an open canvas awaiting the strokes of your aspirations, Alex. What you paint today molds the masterpiece that will grace the canvases of tomorrow."

Chapter LIX: The Dream of Parenthood

As success continued to grace my endeavors, a new aspiration emerged—a longing for the joys of parenthood. This dream, once relegated to the sidelines during the arduous climb of entrepreneurship, now took center stage.

Alex (contemplative): "I can picture our abode resonating with the innocent laughter and footsteps of little ones, Sarah."

Sarah (supportive): "It's a beautiful dream, Alex. Let it mature like a fine wine; we'll savor it when the time is ripe."

Chapter LX: The Burden of Responsibility

Amidst the tapestry of success, the looming prospect of parenthood unfurled a new chapter, weaving intricate patterns of responsibility and contemplation within the room that bore witness to my journey.

Alex (contemplative): "The mantle of parenthood is significant, Sarah. Can I juggle the demands of nurturing a family alongside the responsibilities of my business?"

Sarah (comforting): "Many entrepreneurs have borne this dual mantle with grace, Alex. We'll navigate this path together."

Chapter LXI: The Path to Parenthood

In the grand tapestry of existence, the decision to tread the path to parenthood marked a novel chapter, woven with the threads of optimism and eager expectation. Within the confines of the familiar room, reverberated the unwavering resolve not solely to foster a prosperous business but also to nurture a flourishing family.

Alex (determined): "I aspire to cultivate a family filled with love, Sarah, akin to the triumphs I've sown in my business."

Sarah (joyful): "Hand in hand, we'll traverse the unexplored realms of parenthood, Alex."

Chapter LXII: The Odyssey of Parenthood

Amidst the gentle echoes of our home, a new chapter unfolded – the odyssey of parenthood. The room, once a sanctuary of innovation, now embraced the symphony of laughter and lullabies, marking the rhythm of our transformative journey.

Alex (grateful): "In the tapestry of parenthood, I find gratitude for the lessons and the boundless love it brings, Sarah."

Sarah (reflective): "Our shared odyssey, written in the whispers of family moments, continues to paint a beautiful legacy, Alex."

Chapter LXIII: The Blessing of New Horizons

As the cherished journey of our family expanded, it brought with it the blessing of new horizons. The room, once a silent witness, now echoed with the giggles of innocence and the harmonious cadence of shared moments.

Alex (grateful): "This room holds the magic of beginnings, Sarah. Our family is a treasure beyond measure."

Sarah (content): "In the tapestry of our legacy, new threads of joy and togetherness weave a story of endless blessings, Alex."

Chapter LXiV: The Tapestry of Fulfillment

As the threads of family and business interwove, a tapestry of fulfillment unfolded. The room, once a silent observer, now bore witness to the vibrant hues of a life richly lived.

Alex (content): "Our journey, Sarah, it's creating a tapestry of joy and accomplishment. I couldn't be more fulfilled."

Sarah (grateful): "Our room, our life – a masterpiece woven with threads of love and purpose, Alex."

Chapter LXV: The Timeless Heritage

As the pages of my life unfold, I realize that the true legacy lies in the moments shared, the love cultivated, and the bonds that withstand the tests of time. My room, once a witness to solitude and ambition, is now a sanctuary of enduring familial warmth.

Alex (reflective): "In the end, it's not just about the business deals, but the laughter echoing through these walls."

Sarah (nostalgic): "Our legacy is woven into the fabric of family, Alex. It's a tale of love that transcends the pages of time."

Chapter LXVI: The Uncharted Odyssey

As I stood on the precipice of the future, the room, a steadfast companion throughout my odyssey, whispered promises of undiscovered realms. The uncharted path before me seemed to invite a new story, waiting to be etched on the pages of time.

Alex (reflective): "The horizon stretches endlessly, Sarah. Each step forward unravels a narrative yet untold."

Sarah (inquisitive): "What do you perceive on the unmarked canvases of tomorrow, Alex?"

In the quietude of possibility, with quill in hand, I embark on this unwritten odyssey, embracing the allure of the unknown and weaving the fabric of a legacy that transcends the confines of yesterday.

Chapter LXVIII: The Bonds That Endure

As the years passed, I marveled at the resilience of family bonds. The room, a silent observer of our journey, stood witness to the ebb and flow of life—the celebrations, the trials, and the unbreakable ties that held us together.

Alex (reflective): "Our journey has been a tapestry of moments, Sarah. The room has seen it all."

Sarah (smiling): "And it will continue to, Alex. Our story is still unfolding."

Chapter LXIX: The Lessons of Equilibrium

In the ever-shifting tapestry of life, finding equilibrium between the demands of work and the joys of family emerged as a continuous lesson. The room, once a sanctuary of introspection, now resonated with the laughter and innocence of little ones, symbolizing the perpetual evolution of life's chapters.

Alex (reflective): "It's a delicate dance, Sarah, orchestrating the harmony between career and family. Yet, every step carries a profound significance."

Sarah (acknowledging): "Our journey unfolds with lessons that shape us, Alex."

Chapter LXIX: The Tides of Emotion

In the ebb and flow of daily life, our family found itself navigating the unpredictable currents of emotion. The room, once a silent witness, now echoed with the sentiments of love and longing.

Alex (reflective): "The tides of emotion are like the waves of the sea, Sarah. Sometimes gentle, sometimes turbulent, but always a force to be respected."

Sarah (resolute): "And just as the sea finds balance, so will we, Alex. Our love will be the anchor that steadies us through the emotional tides."

Chapter LXX: The Intricate Symphony

In the intricate symphony of life, I navigated the delicate balance between family and career. The room, a silent witness to the harmonies and discord of my choices, resonated with the melodies of love and ambition.

Alex (contemplative): "Life is a complex composition, Sarah. Each note, a decision shaping our path, and I aim to create a beautiful melody for our family."

Sarah (supportive): "Together, we'll orchestrate a symphony that reflects the richness of both our personal and professional lives."

Chapter LXXI: The Tapestry of Affection

In the delicate dance of daily life, I discovered the art of crafting a tapestry of affection that spanned beyond mere words. The room, a silent witness to my endeavors, embraced the gentle intricacies of love woven into the fabric of our shared moments.

Alex (contemplative): "Love reveals itself not just in grand declarations but in the subtle stitches of our actions. Each moment, a thread binding our hearts together."

Sarah (smiling): "Our family's tapestry is a masterpiece, Alex, adorned with the threads of love we've carefully woven."

Chapter LXXII: The Shared Moments

As the years passed, I discovered the profound joy in cherishing shared moments with my children. The room, once a solitary space, now became a theater for creating beautiful memories.

Alex (smiling): "It's not just about being there, but about truly being present in these shared moments."

Sarah (warmly): "These moments weave the tapestry of a lifetime, Alex."

As the day unfolded, the room awaited the silent reunion, where the echoes of joy and the warmth of familial embrace would once again fill the space.

Alex (softly):"Coming back to you is like finding a piece of my heart I didn't know was missing."

Child 1 (grinning):"Welcome home, Daddy!"

Chapter LXXIII: The Unseen Bonds

In the quiet moments of our lives, the room became a sanctuary for the unseen bonds that tied our family together. It was a space where shared glances spoke volumes, where unspoken understanding bridged the gaps, and where love, though intangible, was undeniably present.

Alex (contemplative): "There's a strength in the bonds that go beyond what words can express, Sarah. It's the foundation of our family."

Sarah (reflective): "Indeed, Alex. This room holds the echoes of our journey, a testament to the enduring ties that bind us together."

And so, the legacy of our family continued to unfold, anchored in the unseen bonds that stood the test of time.

Chapter LXXIV: The Eternal Connection

In the rhythm of life's melodies, the familial bond that enveloped us remained as enduring as the ancient mountains. The room, once a silent observer of aspirations and metamorphoses, cradled the symphony of shared joys and challenges that painted the canvas of our family's story.

Alex (reflective): "Our bond is the essence that threads through the tapestry of our days, Sarah. A resilient tie that time can't erode."

Sarah (grateful): "It's a connection that flourishes, Alex, an everlasting legacy that transcends the pages of our journey."

Chapter LXXV: The Essence of Togetherness

As the pursuit of presence became a guiding principle in my life, the room witnessed a transformation. It turned into a haven for shared activities, where the essence of togetherness blossomed in the simplicity of everyday moments.

Alex (joyful): "Our time together is more precious than gold, Sarah. Let's create a legacy of love and togetherness."

Sarah (smiling): "In these moments, we'll find the true richness of life, Alex."

Chapter LXXVI: The Harmonious Balance

In the pursuit of a harmonious schedule, I realized the importance of intentional choices and mindful planning. The room, once a realm of solitary productivity, transformed into a sanctuary where the delicate balance between work and family life was carefully orchestrated.

Alex (reflective): "Every moment dedicated to work or family holds significance. It's about finding the rhythm that makes our lives harmonious."

Sarah (content): "Our journey to balance has added a beautiful melody to our family life, Alex."

Chapter LXXVII: The Intentional Presence

In my pursuit of a harmonious schedule, I learned the art of intentional presence. The room, witness to my evolving understanding, now stood as a sanctuary for moments deliberately crafted with my family.

Alex (mindful): "It's not just about being there; it's about being present in each moment, cherishing the time we have together."

Sarah (grateful): "Our family thrives on the intentionality of your presence, Alex."

Chapter LXXVIII: The Adventures of Togetherness

In the pursuit of intentional presence, our family embraced a new chapter of shared experiences and adventures. The room, once a quiet refuge, now echoed with the laughter and tales of our togetherness.

Alex (enthusiastic): "Every adventure strengthens the bonds that hold us together, Sarah."

Sarah (elated): "These moments are the building blocks of a lifetime of cherished memories, Alex."

Chapter LXXIX: The Essence of Simplicity

In my pursuit of a balanced life, I discovered the profound beauty within life's simplest joys. The room, once filled with the complexities of ambition, now resonated with the tranquility of simplicity.

Alex (content): "There's a richness in the simplicity of our moments, Sarah. It's in those quiet times that we find true happiness."

Sarah (appreciative): "Simplicity becomes the brush that paints the most vivid strokes on the canvas of our lives."

Chapter LXXX: The Enduring Tapestry

As I sit in the room that has been both witness and stage to my life's odyssey, I find solace in the idea that our legacy is a tapestry woven with the threads of resilience, love, and the pursuit of a meaningful existence.

Alex (contemplative): "Every choice, every challenge, and every triumph adds a new strand to the tapestry of our journey."

Sarah (reflective): "It's a masterpiece, Alex, crafted from the fabric of our shared experiences and the love that binds us."

In this room, where dreams were conceived and realities faced, I realize that life's enduring tapestry is a reflection of the choices we make, the connections we forge, and the profound impact of a life lived with purpose.

Chapter LXXXI: The Blossoming Connection

Amidst the ever-unfolding chapters of our lives, the connection with our children continued to blossom. The room, once a silent observer, now echoed with the laughter and shared stories of a family united.

Alex (grateful): "Our bond is like a blossoming flower, Sarah. Each petal represents a moment, and together, they create a beautiful whole."

Sarah (joyful): "It's a garden of love, Alex, and our family is thriving in its midst."

Chapter LXXXII: The Illuminating Path

In the pursuit of illuminating financial wisdom, I embarked on a journey of insightful lessons with our children. The room, once a haven of ambition, transformed into a classroom of practical knowledge.

Alex (teaching): "Earning, saving, and investing wisely are like building blocks, kids. Let me show you how they create a strong foundation for the future."

Sarah (appreciative): "You're giving them tools that will last a lifetime, Alex."

Chapter LXXXIII: The Inquisitive Minds

As our children's curiosity about money grew, I found myself facing a multitude of inquisitive minds eager to unravel the mysteries of finances. The room, once a place of solitude, transformed into an intellectual hub for exploration.

Child 2 (inquiring): "Mommy, how does money even work? Why do people want it so much?"

Sarah (smiling): "Those are great questions, sweetheart. Let's embark on a journey to uncover the secrets of money together."

Chapter LXXXIV: The Path of Responsibility

In our journey to impart financial wisdom, we forged a path of responsibility through the introduction of a chore chart. This visual roadmap, displayed prominently in the room that once echoed with dreams, now became a guide for our children on their journey to understanding the connection between effort and reward.

Alex (inspiring): "Completing your chores isn't just a task; it's a step on the path to learning about responsibility and the value it brings."

Sarah (nurturing): "It's a meaningful way for them to grasp the importance of contributing to our family, Alex."

Chapter LXXXV: The Thrifty Wisdom

In the pursuit of teaching our children the art of financial wisdom, the room transformed into a haven for valuable lessons. The air was filled with the essence of thriftiness, as I endeavored to instill the importance of mindful spending.

Alex (wise): "In every coin saved lies the potential for future abundance, my dear. Thriftiness is a timeless virtue that paves the way for enduring prosperity."

Child 2 (curious): "What does 'thriftiness' mean, Daddy?"

Alex (smiling): "It means making thoughtful choices with

our money, cherishing what we have, and preparing for the adventures life presents."

As our children grew, so did their curiosity about growing money. The room, once a witness to my personal and professional journey, now became a setting for introducing them to the concept of investments.

Alex (educating): "Investing is like planting a garden. With careful choices, your money can grow and provide returns over time."

Child 1 (intrigued): "Can we really make money grow, Daddy?"

Chapter LXXXVI: The Prudent Choices

Guiding our children through the realm of financial decisions, we emphasized the importance of making prudent choices. The room, once a backdrop for dreams and growth, now served as a platform for instilling a sense of responsibility.

Alex (wisdom): "Every choice you make with your money shapes your financial future. Choose wisely, and your wealth will grow."

Sarah (supportive): "Prudent choices today pave the way for prosperity tomorrow."

As our children grew, so did their curiosity about the world of finance. The room, once a haven for solitude and reflection, now echoed with discussions about wealth, investments, and the value of knowledge.

Alex (enlightening): "Understanding how money works is like unlocking a treasure chest of opportunities. It's not just about what you earn but what you learn."

Sarah (encouraging): "Knowledge truly is wealth, Alex. Let's continue to nurture their curiosity."

Chapter LXXXVII: The Sharing Principle

We instilled the principle of sharing as a cornerstone of financial wisdom. The room, once a backdrop for ambition, now became a stage for teaching empathy.

Alex (empathetic): "Using our money to help others who may be less fortunate is a meaningful way to make a positive impact."

Child 1 (compassionate): "That sounds like a nice thing to do, Daddy."

To reinforce the values of gratitude and appreciation, we introduced a family gratitude journal. The room, once a space for solitude and ambition, now transformed into a hub for cultivating thankfulness.

Alex (encouraging): "Let's take a moment each day to write down something we're thankful for. It helps us appreciate the blessings in our lives."

Sarah (appreciative): "Gratitude is a powerful force that enriches our hearts."

Chapter LXXXVIII: The Stirring Emotions

Teaching our children the principles of money management evoked a spectrum of emotions—patience, understanding, and a burgeoning sense of responsibility.

Alex (reflective): "It transcends mere currency, Sarah. It's about embedding values that will sculpt their futures."

Sarah (proud): "From your guidance, they're imbibing crucial life lessons, Alex."

Chapter LXXXIX: The Enduring Legacy

As the pages of my life turned, I contemplated the enduring legacy I would leave behind. The room, witness to the chapters of my story, resonated with the echoes of choices made and the impact created.

Alex (contemplative): "Our legacy, Sarah, is not just about wealth or achievements. It's about the values and love we've woven into the fabric of our family."

Sarah (reflective): "Indeed, Alex. Our enduring legacy is a testament to a life well-lived, marked by love, wisdom, and the richness of shared moments."

Chapter XC: The Eternal Echo

As time unfurls its chapters, the wisdom embedded in our family's legacy becomes an eternal echo. The room, a silent witness to our endeavors, resonates with the enduring principles that transcend the ages.

Alex (contemplative): "The wisdom we've cultivated is a beacon, Sarah, guiding our family through the boundless expanse of time."

Sarah (reflective): "In each lesson learned and passed down, our legacy becomes an everlasting flame, illuminating the path for generations to come."

Chapter XCI: The Harmonious Balance

In the intricate dance of parenthood, I found myself striving for a harmonious balance between protection and allowing our children the space to forge their paths. The room, once a witness to dreams and aspirations, now harbored the nuanced discussions of guiding our children through life's uncharted territories.

Alex (reflective): "It's a delicate dance, Sarah, ensuring their safety while giving them the freedom to explore."

Sarah (considerate): "Indeed, Alex. Like a well-played melody, finding the right balance requires both caution and liberation."

Chapter XCII: The Unsettled Liberation

As I navigated the path of allowing our children more freedom, a sense of disquiet settled within me. The room, once a sanctuary of ambitions, now resonated with the internal struggle of letting go.

Alex (uneasy): "Granting them independence feels disconcerting, Sarah. What if they face challenges beyond their capacity?"

Sarah (soothing): "Challenges are the forge of resilience, Alex. We'll stand by them, fostering strength in adversity."

Chapter XCIII: The Blooming Autonomy

In the midst of our children's journey into independence, I marveled at the flowering of their autonomy. The room, a once bustling center of business, now stood witness to the quiet transformation, a tableau of their evolving narratives.

Alex (contemplative): "They're forging their paths, Sarah, stepping into the world with purpose."

Sarah (reflective): "Our guidance has cultivated seeds of resilience. Now, they face the world's challenges with a strength uniquely their own."

Chapter XCIV: The

Unfolding Chapters

As the seasons changed, so did the chapters of our family's story. The room, a silent witness to our journey, held the echoes of laughter, tears, and the unwavering bond that defined us.

Alex (reflective): "Every moment, every challenge, has shaped our story, Sarah. I wouldn't change a single page."

Sarah (smiling): "Our story is a masterpiece, Alex. And the best chapters are yet to unfold."

And so, with hearts intertwined, we eagerly turned the pages of the unwritten chapters, embracing the ever-unfolding tapestry of our family's legacy.

Chapter XCV: The Letting Go

In the golden corridors of life, where each step echoes the footsteps of time, I stumbled upon a truth both ancient and enduring—the art of letting go. It was not a singular moment, but an eternal dance with the cosmos, a melody played on the strings of fate.

The room, once adorned with the tapestries of my desires, transformed into a temple of introspection. The flickering candlelight whispered secrets of surrender, as shadows danced along the walls—a silent testimony to the continuous process of release.

As I gazed upon the relics of yesteryears, memories etched in the very fabric of the space, I embraced the understanding that letting go is not an act of abandonment. It is a symphony of trust played in the heartstrings of destiny.

Alex (contemplative): "Letting go, my dear Sarah, is an ancient alchemy. It is the transmutation of attachment into the elixir of freedom. A relinquishment not of love but of the need to control."

Sarah (profound): "In the grand theater of life, we are both actors and spectators. Letting go is the acknowledgment that our fellow players have their own script, their own stage. We release them to perform their own masterpiece."

In the silence that followed, the room embraced the wisdom shared—a sanctuary of profound realizations. For in the letting go, we discover not only the freedom of others but the liberation of our own souls. And so, in this sacred chamber, we continued our journey—ever trusting, ever releasing, ever becoming.

Chapter XCVI: The Legacy of Trust

In the perennial garden of life, where the seeds of character are sown and nurtured, a new chapter blossomed—an ode to the evolution of virtue, the enduring pillar of trust, and the familial bonds that intertwine our destinies. The room, once a sanctuary echoing with the whispers of aspirations, now stood as a shrine to the profound trust vested in the hearts of our progeny.

Alex (gratitude etched in every word): "Within the vaults of our trust, my dearest Sarah, lies a silent symphony—an unspoken testament to the depths of our love."

Sarah (unwavering in her certainty): "Indeed, Alex. As they traverse the labyrinthine passages of life, our children shall carry this sacred legacy of trust as a compass, steering them through the tempests with unwavering resilience."

In the hallowed silence that followed, the room absorbed the resonance of shared wisdom—a legacy not inscribed on parchment but etched in the very fabric of our existence. For within the crucible of trust, we forged not only familial bonds but an enduring testament to the essence of our shared journey. And so, under the celestial canopy of trust, our legacy continued to unfurl—a tapestry woven with the golden threads of love, character, and the timeless legacy of trust.

Chapter XCVII: The Ever-Expanding Horizons

In the grand tapestry of existence, where each thread intertwines with destiny, a new chapter unfurled—the saga of our children venturing into the boundless realms of the world. The room, keeper of our familial chronicles, stood as a silent witness to the odyssey we embarked upon as a united front.

Alex (satisfied): "Their destinies are painted on the canvas of limitless potential, Sarah. I eagerly anticipate the kaleidoscope of experiences that await them."

Sarah (hopeful): "With our love as their compass and our guidance as the wind beneath their wings, they shall soar to heights unknown, Alex."

As the echoes of these sentiments lingered in the room, it resonated not only with the promise of tomorrow but with the profound understanding that, even as horizons expanded, the roots of our familial bonds would forever anchor us in the soil of shared love and enduring unity. And so, under the ever-expanding canopy of possibilities, our familial odyssey continued—a journey marked by the limitless horizons of life.

Chapter XCVIII: The First Day of School

In the chronicles of growing up, where each chapter unfolds a new page of discovery, a milestone emerged—the inaugural step into the realm of education. The room, witness to the evolution of solitude into shared ambitions, now embraced the lively chaos of backpacks and the promise of scholastic beginnings.

Alex (filled with encouragement): "This is the start of a wondrous journey, my little scholars. Embrace the learning, and let kindness be your guide."

Sarah (infused with reassurance): "As you step into the world of knowledge, remember that we eagerly await your return, ready to hear tales of your adventures and triumphs."

And so, as the school bell rang and the echoes of excited chatter filled the room, it marked not just the commencement of academic pursuits but the continuation of a familial saga—a narrative where each chapter, whether in solitude or shared moments, contributed to the tapestry of our ever-unfolding story.

Chapter XCIX: The Homework Dilemma

In the rhythmic cadence of our daily lives, a chapter unfolded—one that echoed the familiar notes of homework assignments and the scholarly pursuit of knowledge. The room, previously a bustling center of business activities, transformed into a sanctuary for academic endeavors.

Alex (overflowing with support): "The adventure of learning awaits us, my little scholars. Let's dive into these assignments together, where every challenge is an opportunity for growth."

Child 1 (brimming with determination): "I'm ready to give it my all, Daddy!"

And so, amidst the quiet hum of concentration and the scribbling of pencils, the room bore witness to not just the completion of assignments but to the bonds forged through shared intellectual pursuits. In this haven of study and collaboration, the pages of our familial narrative turned, marking a chapter where the pursuit of knowledge became a shared odyssey.

Chapter C: The Friendships and Challenges

In the grand tapestry of social bonds, where threads of friendship and challenges interweave, a significant chapter unfolded. Our children, navigating the intricate landscapes of school life, discovered the nuances of camaraderie and the complexities of interpersonal dynamics. The room, a witness to ambitions, now served as a haven for the contemplation of these shared experiences.

Alex (imbued with empathy): "Friendships are like constellations in the night sky—beautiful, yet intricate. If challenges arise, remember, we're here to navigate the celestial map together."

Sarah (overflowing with compassion): "Whether it's laughter shared with friends or the weight of challenges faced, our ears are open, ready to listen and support, no matter the tales you bring."

As the room echoed with the stories of friendships blossoming and the trials encountered, it marked not only a chapter but a testament to the resilience of familial bonds— a narrative where every shared experience, joy, or hardship contributed to the mosaic of our family's collective journey.

Chapter CI: The Parent-Teacher Meetings

In the continuum of our commitment to education, a chapter unfolded—the symbiotic relationship between home and school encapsulated in parent-teacher meetings. The room, a former sanctuary of inspiration, now embraced the role of a space for earnest discussions on progress and challenges.

Alex (wholeheartedly engaged): "Our presence here echoes our dedication to their learning journey, Sarah. Let's forge a collaborative alliance with their teachers."

Sarah (resolute): "Education is a partnership, and our commitment to their growth is unwavering. Together, we navigate this voyage."

As the room echoed with conversations that resonated not only with academic reports but with shared aspirations, it marked not just a chapter but a testament to the strength of the triad—parents, teachers, and students—a harmonious chord in the symphony of educational endeavors.

Chapter CII: The Stress of Exams

In the seasonal rhythm of academia, a chapter unfurled— a narrative of stress and pressure as exams loomed on the horizon. The room, a witness to dreams and growth, now transformed into a refuge for navigating the challenges posed by academic assessments.

Alex (soothing): "Exams are like storms that test the resilience of your knowledge, my dear ones. Face them with courage, and know that we stand proudly behind you."

Child 2 (expressing nervousness): "I'm scared, Daddy."

As the room absorbed the palpable tension and the unspoken fears, it marked not merely a chapter but a reminder of the fragility of youthful apprehensions and the steadfast support woven into the fabric of family—the pillar that stands unwavering amid the tempest of academic trials.

Chapter CIII: The Importance of Resilience

In the crucible of life's challenges, a chapter unfolded— an exploration of resilience and the unwavering resolve to persist in the face of adversity. The room, once adorned with dreams, now stood as a workshop for the forging of character.

Alex (filled with encouragement): "Mistakes are the stepping stones to mastery, my dear ones. Embrace them, learn from them, and let resilience be the guiding light through every trial."

Sarah (imbued with support): "You possess an inner strength that transcends obstacles, my cherished ones. In the face of adversity, remember, you are capable of surmounting anything."

As the room resonated with the echoes of these empowering sentiments, it marked not just a chapter but a testament to the fortitude embedded in the heart of our familial narrative—a legacy of resilience and the enduring spirit that propels us forward on the journey of life.

Chapter CIV: The Celebrations of Achievements

In the symphony of life's milestones, a chapter gracefully unfolded—a chronicle of celebrating the triumphs, both grand and subtle, achieved by our beloved children. The room, once a refuge of solitude, now resonated with the exuberance of accomplishments.

Alex (brimming with pride): "Your unwavering dedication and hard work deserve every celebration, my dear ones. Continue to reach for the stars, for your potential knows no bounds."

Sarah (overflowing with elation): "In every achievement, we witness the testament of your resolute spirit. Your determination lights the path to success."

As the room echoed with the joyous reverberations of celebration, it marked not merely a chapter but a perpetual ode to the resilience and tenacity embedded in the fabric of our familial tapestry—a celebration of victories, both big and small, that adorn the journey of our shared existence.

Chapter CV: The Legacy of Learning

In the perpetual dance of life's evolution, a new chapter unfolded—a testament to the transformative power of character, the profound significance of education, and the steadfast support that defined our familial bonds. The room, once a cradle of dreams and growth, now stood as an emblem of the everlasting odyssey of learning.

Alex (filled with gratitude): "Through the corridors of education, we've paved the way for a luminous future, Sarah."

Sarah (brimming with hope): "The love of learning, woven into the very fabric of their being, will accompany them on their lifelong journey, Alex."

As the room absorbed the echoes of these sentiments, it marked not just a chapter but a legacy—a legacy of character, education, and unwavering support that would continue to resonate through the generations of our familial saga.

Chapter CVI: The Ever-Expanding Knowledge

In the eternal pursuit of wisdom, a chapter gracefully unfolded—a narrative of our children's ongoing educational journey and the boundless expansion of their knowledge. The room, a silent witness to a myriad of tales, now echoed with the importance of cultivating young minds.

Alex (filled with contentment): "Their insatiable curiosity and the continual quest for knowledge will be their guiding stars, Sarah. The tapestry of their futures is poised to unfold in remarkable ways."

Sarah (brimming with optimism): "We stand at the ready to lend our unwavering support and to revel in the joy of every discovery they make, Alex."

As the room embraced the echoes of these sentiments, it marked not just a chapter but an acknowledgment of the perpetual evolution of understanding—an ever-expanding journey of knowledge that would shape the destinies of our beloved children.

Chapter CVII: The Friendships We Choose

In the intricate tapestry of growing up, a chapter unfolded —an exploration of the nuanced art of choosing friends. The room, once a haven of solitude and ambition, now hosted pivotal conversations about the significance of friendship.

Alex (expressing concern): "Choosing friends wisely is a compass for navigating life, kids. Surround yourselves with those who uplift and inspire."

Sarah (infused with support): "Friendship weaves the threads of our life stories. We're here to guide you towards positive connections and enriching experiences."

As the room absorbed the weight of these conversations, it marked not just a chapter but a discourse on the importance of cultivating friendships that contribute to the tapestry of a fulfilling and harmonious life journey.

Chapter CVIII: The Warning Signs

In the realm of life's lessons, a chapter unfolded—an exploration of the crucial awareness of warning signs in friendships. The room, formerly a hub of business activities, now transformed into a stage for discussions about the intricate dynamics of relationships.

Alex (imparting wisdom): "Recognizing warning signs, like peer pressure and negativity, is pivotal. If your friends are pushing you beyond your comfort zone, it's a signal to pause and reflect."

Child 1 (expressing curiosity): "What do we do if that happens, Daddy?"

Alex (offering guidance): "In those moments, my dear, it's essential to trust your instincts. Open up to us about your feelings, and together, we'll navigate the best course of action. Healthy friendships are built on understanding, respect, and mutual support."

As the room absorbed the weight of these conversations, it marked not just a chapter but a commitment to fostering resilience and empowering our children with the tools to navigate the complex landscapes of relationships.

Chapter CIX: The Importance of Self-Respect

In the sanctum of personal growth, a chapter gracefully unfolded—an exploration of the paramount importance of self-respect and the art of standing firm in one's authenticity. The room, once a sanctuary of inspiration, now evolved into a crucible for nurturing confidence.

Alex (instilling empowerment): "Your individuality is a treasure, my dear ones. Never compromise your true self to conform with others. Embrace the strength that comes from self-respect."

Sarah (filled with encouragement): "You are a mosaic of unique qualities, each piece contributing to the masterpiece that is you. Stand tall, for your authenticity is a beacon of light."

As the room resonated with these empowering affirmations, it marked not merely a chapter but a dedication to cultivating a sense of self-respect—a cornerstone for navigating the complexities of friendships and relationships with unwavering confidence.

Chapter CX: The Difficult Decisions

In the saga of growing up, a chapter unfolded—an exploration of the challenging decisions our children encountered regarding friendships that no longer resonated with their well-being. The room, once a stage for ambition, now transformed into a haven for soul-searching.

Alex (infused with compassion): "Choosing to part ways with friendships that no longer bring joy is a brave decision, my dear. It's an act of self-care and growth."

Child 2 (expressing reflection): "But it's hard, Daddy."

Alex (supportive): "Indeed, my little one, it is hard. Change, especially in relationships, can be challenging. But remember, your happiness and well-being matter. We're here to guide you through these moments of difficulty."

As the room absorbed the weight of these heartfelt conversations, it marked not just a chapter but a poignant acknowledgment of the complexities inherent in making decisions that prioritize one's emotional health—a testament to the resilience and wisdom our children were cultivating as they navigated the intricate landscapes of growing up.

Chapter CXI: The Supportive Conversations

In the evolving narrative of our familial journey, a chapter gracefully unfolded—an ode to the multitude of supportive conversations that formed the backbone of understanding and guidance in navigating the intricate realm of friendships. The room, a witness to dreams and growth, now resonated with the echoes of heartfelt discussions.

Alex (providing reassurance): "Your friendships are an integral part of your life, and we want to be your compass in navigating them. Whether the seas are calm or turbulent, you can always share your thoughts with us."

Sarah (overflowing with love): "Every conversation is a bridge connecting us, dear ones. We're here to listen, to understand, and to support you in making choices that nurture your well-being."

As the room absorbed the warmth of these exchanges, it marked not merely a chapter but an enduring commitment to fostering open communication—a foundation for the resilient bonds that defined our family's shared odyssey.

Chapter CXII: The Power of Good Influences

In the tapestry of shared experiences, a chapter unfolded —an acknowledgment and celebration of the positive influences that enriched our children's lives through their friendships. The room, once a haven of solitude, now radiated with the joy born from healthy and uplifting relationships.

Alex (brimming with pride): "Seeing you surrounded by friends who inspire and uplift you fills our hearts with pride. It's a testament to the wonderful individuals you've become."

Sarah (overflowing with gratitude): "These friendships, woven with threads of strength and happiness, are invaluable treasures. We're grateful for the positive influences shaping your journey."

As the room resonated with the echoes of celebration, it marked not merely a chapter but a perpetual ode to the transformative power of good influences—a melody that harmonized with the symphony of our family's collective narrative.

Chapter CXIII: The Legacy of Choosing Wisely

In the ever-unfolding tapestry of our narrative, a new chapter gracefully unfurled—a testament to the cultivation of character, the discernment in choosing friends wisely, and the enduring support that sculpted the essence of our family. The room, once a realm of dreams and growth, now stood as a symbol of the values ingrained in our children.

Alex (filled with gratitude): "The values we've shared have become a compass guiding them to make wise choices in friendships, Sarah."

Sarah (brimming with hope): "As they embark on their individual journeys, those values will be their North Star, lighting the path throughout their lives, Alex."

As the room absorbed the echoes of these sentiments,

it marked not just a chapter but a legacy—a legacy of character, discernment, and familial support that would reverberate through the generations of our family's timeless saga.

Chapter CXIV: The Ever-Evolving Friendships

In the perpetual ebb and flow of friendships, a chapter gracefully unfolded—an acknowledgment of the ongoing journey our children embarked upon in navigating the intricate tapestry of social connections. The room, a silent witness to myriad tales, now stood as a poignant reminder of the significance of embracing positive influences.

Alex (filled with contentment): "As their friendships weave through the chapters of life, Sarah, they'll glean valuable lessons and emerge stronger."

Sarah (brimming with optimism): "Our role as guides and pillars of support remains unwavering. With every twist and turn, we'll be there to lend our wisdom and encouragement, Alex."

As the room absorbed the echoes of these assurances, it marked not just a chapter but an affirmation of the ever-evolving nature of friendships—a testament to the resilience and growth embedded in the heart of our familial narrative.

Chapter CXV: The Complex World of Cash Flow

In the realm of parental challenges, a chapter unfolded—one marked by the intricacies of imparting financial wisdom to our children. The room, once a refuge of solitude and ambition, transformed into a classroom for the vital lessons of financial education.

Alex (engaging in explanation): "Cash flow, my dear ones, is like the ebb and flow of money in a business, akin to the currents in a river. It's about managing the inflow and outflow to keep things running smoothly."

Child 1 (expressing confusion): "But why is it important, Daddy?"

Alex (elaborating): "Great question! Just like a river needs a balanced flow to sustain its ecosystem, a business—or even our household—requires a balanced cash flow. It ensures we have enough to cover our expenses, invest in opportunities, and weather any unexpected challenges."

Child 1 (curious): "So, it's like making sure the money doesn't run out, right?"

Alex (smiling): "Exactly! It's about maintaining a healthy financial flow so we can achieve our goals, whether it's saving for the future, supporting our lifestyle, or seizing opportunities that come our way."

As the room absorbed the conversations about the complexities of cash flow, it marked not just a chapter but a commitment to providing our children with the tools to navigate the intricate waters of financial responsibility.

Chapter CXVI: The Concept of Fiat Currency

In the pursuit of financial literacy, a chapter gracefully unfolded—an exploration into the concept of fiat currency and its pivotal role in the economic landscape. The room, once a bustling hub of business activities, now set the stage for conversations delving into the very essence of money.

Alex (breaking it down): "Think of fiat currency as a kind of agreement, kids. The government says, 'This piece of paper or this digital number represents a certain value, and you can use it to trade for goods and services.'"

Sarah (enthusiastic): "It's the backbone of our economic system, a tool that allows people to exchange value and keep the wheels of society turning."

As the room absorbed the simplicity in the explanation, it marked not just a chapter but a commitment to demystifying complex financial concepts for our children —a foundation for understanding the mechanics of the economic world they would inherit.

Chapter CXVII: The Basics of How Businesses Work

In the tapestry of financial education, a chapter unfolded—a venture into unraveling the complexities of how businesses operated. The room, once a sanctuary of inspiration, now transformed into a haven for simplifying intricate concepts into digestible nuggets of understanding.

Alex (with patience): "Imagine businesses as giant puzzles, my dear ones. They piece together products or services that people want or need and then exchange them for money."

Child 2 (expressing curiosity): "But how do they make money, Daddy?"

Alex (explaining): "Great question! Businesses make money

by selling their products or services at a price that covers the cost of making those products or offering those services. The difference between what they earn and what they spend is their profit."

Child 2 (nodding): "So, the more people who buy from them, the more money they make?"

Alex (smiling): "Exactly! When businesses provide something that people value, and they do it well, more people want to buy from them. That's how they grow and thrive."

As the room absorbed these conversations about the basics of how businesses operate, it marked not just a chapter but a commitment to fostering a foundational understanding of economic principles for our children—an investment in their ability to navigate the intricate landscape of the business world.

Chapter CXVIII: The Emotional Impact of Financial Concepts

In the realm of financial education, a chapter gracefully unfolded—an exploration into the emotional nuances that accompanied the journey of understanding complex financial concepts. The room, once a realm of dreams and growth, now became a sanctuary for nurturing emotional intelligence intertwined with financial literacy.

Alex (empathizing): "Learning about finances can bring up various feelings, from curiosity to confusion and maybe even a bit of anxiety. It's okay to feel that way, and we're here to guide you through it."

Sarah (infused with reassurance): "Your emotional

responses are valid, and it's a journey we take together. Building financial literacy is not just about numbers; it's also about understanding how these concepts impact our lives and emotions."

As the room absorbed the emotional undercurrents of financial education, it marked not just a chapter but a commitment to nurturing a holistic understanding—a blend of knowledge and emotional intelligence that would empower our children in their future financial endeavors.

Chapter CXIX: The Sage's Symphony of Wealth

In the intricate tapestry of financial wisdom, our chapter gracefully unfolds—an exploration into the paramount importance of saving, investing, and the ageless teachings reminiscent of "The Richest Man in Babylon." The room, once a sanctuary of solitude, now resonates with discussions that weave the fabric of financial security, guided by the wisdom of ancient scrolls.

Alex (bridging the teachings): "Behold, my dear ones, the harmonious symphony of wealth. Saving and investing are the notes that compose this melodic journey toward a prosperous future."

Child 1 (engaged): "So, it's like the wisdom of Babylon, Daddy?"

Alex (nodding): "Indeed, my child. Much like the wise merchants of Babylon, let us embark on a journey of financial growth. Setting aside money is akin to planting seeds, and wise investing is the art of tending to those seeds, ensuring a bountiful harvest for dreams to blossom."

Child 1 (inspired): "How do we start, Daddy?"

Alex (smiling): "We shall open the gates to financial abundance by exploring avenues beyond mere savings. We'll venture into the realm of judicious investments, diversifying our assets as the sages of old did, ensuring prosperity echoes through the corridors of our tomorrows."

As the room absorbs the wisdom of Babylonian principles intertwined with contemporary understanding, it marks not just a chapter but a symphony—a harmonious blend of ancient guidance and modern practices, orchestrating the wealth-building journey for our children's prosperous futures.

Chapter CXX: The Enduring Echoes of Financial Wisdom

As my narrative weaves through the chapters, it stands as a testament to the evolution of our story—a journey marked by character development, the sanctity of financial education, and the unwavering support defining our familial tapestry. My room, once a realm of dreams and growth, now stands as a symbol of the enduring legacy of knowledge bestowed upon our children.

Alex (filled with gratitude): "In nurturing their financial literacy, we've gifted them a compass for life's journey, Sarah. It's a legacy that will guide them through the twists and turns ahead."

Sarah (infused with hope): "And as they tread their paths, they'll carry these invaluable lessons, passing on the torch of financial wisdom to the generations that follow, Alex."

In the hallowed space of our familial abode, the echoes of financial acumen linger, creating not just a chapter but a legacy—a testament to the enduring power of knowledge that transcends time.

Chapter CXXI: The Unfolding Horizon of Financial Insight

In the chronicles of our familial odyssey, a new chapter unfolds—an exploration into the ever-expanding understanding of finance by our children. The room, a silent witness to myriad tales, stands as a poignant reminder of the profound significance of financial wisdom in shaping their lives.

Alex (filled with contentment): "The canvas of their financial knowledge is just beginning to receive brushstrokes, Sarah. I anticipate with joy the masterpiece they will paint with these lessons."

Sarah (brimming with optimism): "As their understanding deepens, we'll stand as beacons, offering support and guidance through the intricate landscape of financial choices, Alex."

In the sacred space of our home, where stories are etched and wisdom shared, this chapter marks not just a progression but a journey—an expedition into the limitless horizons of financial insight, a legacy unfolding in the pages of our family's narrative.

Chapter CXXII: The Enigma of Fractional Reserve Banking

In the symphony of financial enlightenment, our chapter unfolds—an exploration into the enigmatic realm of fractional reserve banking for our children. The room, once a haven of solitude and ambition, transforms into a classroom, unveiling the mysteries of financial intricacies.

Alex (making it relatable): "Picture this, my dear ones—it's like having a magical jar where we keep some of our money, and the rest is lent out to others in need. Banks operate on a similar principle, just on a grander scale."

Child 1 (intrigued): "Do they really lend out more money than they have?"

Alex (delving into the mystery): "Indeed, they do. It's a fascinating system where banks lend out a fraction of the money they hold, keeping only a portion in reserve. It's like a financial dance that keeps the wheels of the economy turning."

Child 2 (thoughtful): "But Daddy, isn't that like cheating? Lending more than you actually have?"

Alex (explaining with care): "It may seem that way, but in the world of banking, it's a practice designed to facilitate economic growth. It allows more people to access funds for various needs, like buying homes or starting businesses. However, it's essential to understand the balance and responsibility that comes with it."

As the room resonates with questions, it marks not just a chapter but an ongoing dialogue—an exploration into the ethical nuances of financial systems, where understanding becomes a beacon guiding our children through the complex landscape of fiscal responsibility.

Chapter CXXIII: The Fable of Wealth-Building Debts

In the chronicles of financial literacy, a new chapter unfolds —an exploration into the distinctions between good debt and bad debt for our children. The room, once a bustling hub of business activities, transforms into a stage where the narrative of financial decisions takes center spotlight.

Alex (clarifying with wisdom): "Imagine debt as characters in a story, my dear ones. Good debt, akin to a wise ally, helps you build wealth—like taking a loan to buy a house. On the other hand, bad debt, a trickster in disguise, is when you borrow for things that don't grow in value, like fleeting pleasures or unnecessary gadgets."

Sarah (immersing in the lesson): "It's a tale of making astute choices, navigating the twists and turns of financial decisions to sculpt a prosperous future."

As the room absorbs the essence of this financial fable, it marks not just a chapter but an allegory—a journey into the art of discernment, where our children learn to distinguish between the characters of good and bad debt, crafting a narrative of fiscal wisdom in the pages of their financial tales.

Chapter CXXIV: The Symphony of Assets and Liabilities

In the grand orchestration of financial comprehension, a new chapter unfolds—an exploration into the realms of assets and liabilities for our children. The room, once a sanctuary of inspiration, metamorphoses into a canvas where complex ideas are painted with the brushstrokes of creative storytelling.

Alex (painting a vivid picture): "Envision assets as diligent workers in your financial garden, toiling to make you money. On the other side, liabilities are like persistent bills, each one nibbling away at your earnings."

Child 2 (pondering): "So, we aim for a garden full of workers and fewer pesky bills?"

Alex (nodding with a smile): "Precisely, my insightful one. Cultivating a flourishing garden of assets while taming the liabilities is the melody of financial harmony."

As the room resonates with this financial symphony, it marks not just a chapter but a masterpiece—an odyssey into the language of assets and liabilities, where our children learn to compose a financial opus that echoes with the chords of prosperity.

Chapter CXXV: The Odyssey of Passive Prosperity

In the tapestry of financial education, a new chapter unfurls —an expedition into the quest for passive income for our children. The room, once a realm of dreams and growth, transforms into a realm where the concept of money working for you takes center stage.

Alex (painting a vision): "Imagine passive income as a magical money tree, my dear ones. It bestows fruits of wealth upon you without requiring your constant toil."

Child 1 (filled with enthusiasm): "A money tree? That sounds amazing, Daddy! Can I have one?"

Alex (with a twinkle in his eye): "In a way, we can create our own money trees by making smart investment choices. It's a journey toward financial freedom, where our money works for us, allowing us to enjoy the fruits of our labor without being tied to the daily grind."

As the room absorbs the allure of passive prosperity, it marks not just a chapter but an odyssey—an adventure into the realms of financial independence, where our children learn the art of letting money grow and flourish, echoing the sweet fruits of a well-nurtured money tree.

Chapter CXXVI: The Harmony of Three Incomes - Effort, Investment, and Freedom

In the symphony of financial enlightenment, a new chapter unfolds—an introduction to the trio of income for our children. The room, once a place of solitude, transforms into a forum where discussions about financial independence echo through its walls.

Alex (shedding light): "Think of it as a trio, my dear ones. Labor income is the melody of your hard work, the tune of a job well done. Portfolio income, a harmonious note, arrives from wise investments like stocks. Lastly, passive income, the sweet refrain, is the reward for letting your money work diligently for you."

Sarah (instilling balance): "It's a composition of balance, weaving together the efforts of work, the wisdom of investments, and the freedom that passive income brings."

As the room resonates with the melody of these three

incomes, it marks not just a chapter but a symphony —an orchestration of financial understanding, where our children learn to conduct the harmony of labor, portfolio, and passive income, creating a melody that leads them towards the crescendo of financial independence.

Chapter CXXVII: The Puzzle of Taxes and The Quest for Tax Efficiency

In the ever-unfolding tapestry of financial education, a dual chapter emerges—an exploration into the enigma of taxes and the subsequent quest for tax efficiency for our children. The room, once a realm of dreams, undergoes a metamorphosis, transforming into a space where the understanding of taxes takes center stage.

Alex (making it relatable): "Consider taxes as pieces of a puzzle, my curious ones. Each contribution, no matter how small, forms a vital part of supporting our community. It's akin to assembling a mosaic where your financial participation helps build the foundations of schools, hospitals, and roads—essentials that benefit everyone."

Child 2 (inquiring): "But why do we have to pay taxes, Daddy?"

Alex (illuminating the purpose): "Paying taxes is a shared responsibility to ensure our community thrives. It's a way of contributing to the greater good, supporting the services and infrastructure that uplift our society."

As the room absorbs the essence of this tax puzzle, a segue unfolds—a transition into the next chapter.

Chapter CXXVII: The Quest

for Tax Efficiency

The saga of financial literacy continues with a new chapter —an exploration into the quest for tax efficiency for our children. The room, once a haven of dreams, now metamorphoses into a realm where understanding the nuances of taxes becomes a vital part of the narrative.

Alex (unveiling the quest): "Consider the quest for tax efficiency, my inquisitive ones. While we all contribute our fair share, there are strategic ways to manage your finances that might lead to paying less tax."

Child 1 (curious): "Are there really ways to pay less tax, Daddy?"

Alex (revealing the secrets): "Indeed, my insightful one. By making smart financial choices, like taking advantage of tax deductions and credits, investing wisely, and planning for the future, you can optimize your tax situation. It's like navigating a maze where you aim to keep more of your hard-earned money while still fulfilling your civic duty."

As the room resonates with the quest for tax efficiency, it marks not just a chapter but a dual journey—an expedition into the intricacies of civic responsibility and financial strategy, where our children learn to assemble the puzzle pieces of taxes and navigate the twists and turns, seeking efficiency in their fiscal quest.

Chapter CXXVIII: The Ever-Expanding Wisdom

As the chapters of financial wisdom unfold, a new one takes its place—an exploration into the ever-expanding legacy of financial knowledge for our children. The room, once a sanctuary of dreams, now stands as a testament to the evolution of understanding and the enduring support woven into our family's narrative.

Alex (reflective): "Our legacy of financial knowledge is a precious gift, Sarah. It's a beacon guiding our children through the complexities of life."

Sarah (optimistic): "And as they carry this wisdom forward, they become torchbearers, passing the flame to the next generation."

In the room that witnessed the growth of dreams, the legacy of financial knowledge becomes a living testament, echoing with the promise of a brighter, more informed future.

Chapter CXXIX: The Ever-Expanding Financial Horizons

As our children continued to learn about the world of finance, I knew that their horizons would continue to expand. The room, which had witnessed so much, stood as a reminder of the importance of financial wisdom in their lives.

Alex (content): "Their journey of financial knowledge is just beginning, Sarah. I'm excited to see how they apply these lessons."

Sarah (optimistic): "And we'll be here to support and guide them every step of the way, Alex."

Chapter CXXX: The Closing Chapter

As the years passed, our children grew into young adults,

carrying with them the lessons of financial wisdom, resilience, and the values we had instilled in them. The room, once a place of solitude and ambition, had transformed into a sanctuary of cherished memories.

Alex (reflective): "Our journey, Sarah, it's been nothing short of incredible."

Sarah (nostalgic): "From dreams to reality, we've experienced it all together."

Chapter CXXXI: The Legacy We Leave

Our family had come a long way from the modest room where it all began. The room, once a hub of business activities, now stood as a symbol of our growth, love, and the enduring legacy we had created.

Alex (grateful): "Our legacy, it's not just about wealth or success, but the love and values we've passed on."

Sarah (proud): "And the impact we've had on our children and those around us."

Chapter CXXXII: The New Beginnings

Our children had embarked on their own journeys, carrying the torch of our family's values and wisdom. The room, once a sanctuary of inspiration, was now a space for us to embrace new beginnings.

Alex (hopeful): "Their futures are bright, Sarah. It's time for us to embrace this new chapter of our lives."

Sarah (optimistic): "And to see what adventures lie ahead."

Chapter CXXXIII: The Room of Dreams

The room that had witnessed our entire story was now a place of reflection. Its walls echoed with the laughter of our children, the lessons learned, and the love that had filled it.

Alex (content): "This room, Sarah, it holds the heart and soul of our family's journey."

Sarah (smiling): "And it always will."

Chapter CXXXIV: The Legacy Lives On

Our story had reached its final chapter, but our legacy would live on through our children and the generations to come. The room, once a place of dreams and growth, was now a symbol of the love and wisdom we had shared.

Alex (grateful): "Our story, Sarah, it's a testament to the power of family, resilience, and the pursuit of dreams."

Sarah (fulfilled): "And the legacy we leave behind."

Chapter CXXXV: The Ever-Expanding Future

As we looked toward the future, we knew that our family's journey would continue to evolve. The room, which had witnessed so much, stood as a reminder that life was an ever-expanding adventure.

Alex (smiling): "Our story may be ending, but theirs is just beginning."

Sarah (joyful): "And we'll be here to cheer them on every step of the way."

And so, our tale came to an end, but it was not the end of the story. It was the beginning of many new stories, each written by our children as they embarked on their own journeys, guided by the lessons of the room of dreams.

Alex (closing the book): "Goodnight, my love. Our story will live on in the hearts of our children."

Sarah (smiling): "Goodnight, Alex. Our legacy continues to shine bright."

[The room fell into a peaceful silence, a room that had seen dreams turn into reality, a room that had been witness to the extraordinary journey of a family, a room that held the legacy of love and wisdom for generations to come.]

"The End"